Horse
Heroes

FIRST EDITION
Senior Editor Linda Esposito; **Managing Art Editor** Peter Bailey; **US Editor** Regina Kahney;
Production Josie Alabaster; **Picture Researcher** Liz Moore; **Illustrator** Mario Capaldi;
Reading Consultant Linda Gambrell, PhD

THIS EDITION
Editorial Management by Oriel Square
Produced for DK by WonderLab Group LLC
Jennifer Emmett, Erica Green, Kate Hale, *Founders*

Editors Grace Hill Smith, Libby Romero, Michaela Weglinski;
Photography Editors Kelley Miller, Annette Kiesow, Nicole DiMella; **Managing Editor** Rachel Houghton;
Designers Project Design Company; **Researcher** Michelle Harris; **Copy Editor** Lori Merritt;
Indexer Connie Binder; **Proofreader** Larry Shea; **Reading Specialist** Dr. Jennifer L. Albro;
Curriculum Specialist Elaine Larson

Published in the United States by DK Publishing
1745 Broadway, 20th Floor, New York, NY 10019

Copyright © 2023 Dorling Kindersley Limited
DK, a Division of Penguin Random House LLC
23 24 25 26 10 9 8 7 6 5 4 3 2 1
001-334007-June/2023

A catalog record for this book
is available from the Library of Congress.
HC ISBN: 978-0-7440-7330-0
PB ISBN: 978-0-7440-7331-7

DK books are available at special discounts when purchased in bulk for sales promotions, premiums,
fundraising, or educational use. For details, contact: DK Publishing Special Markets,
1745 Broadway, 20th Floor, New York, NY 10019
SpecialSales@dk.com

Printed and bound in China

The publisher would like to thank the following for their kind permission to reproduce their images:
a=above; c=center; b=below; l=left; r=right; t=top; b/g=background

Alamy Stock Photo: China Span / Keren Su 15crb, RGR Collection 21tl, The Print Collector / Ann Ronan Picture Library / Heritage-
Images 7b; **Dreamstime.com:** Kseniya Abramova 40cl, Kseniya Abramova / Tristana 31crb, Ruth Black 42cla, Mitchell Gunn 32b,
Isselee 36tl, Olga Itina 3cb, Lazyllama 31tr, Photoquest 20t, Ricochet69 7tr, Ievgeniia Shugaliia 40tl, Toniflap 15tr;
Getty Images: AFP / Staff / Alexander Klein 24tl, Hulton Archive / Stringer / B. Marshall 31clb, Hulton Archive / Stringer /
Chris Ware 35tl, Hulton Fine Art Collection / Brandstaetter Images 24b, Photodisc / Image Source 33tr, Popperfoto / Ed Lacey 33tl,
/ Rolls Press 30t, Stringer / Jack Taylor 25tr, 26clb, Sygma / Olivier Roques Rogery 27crb; **Getty Images / iStock:** E+ / CasarsaGuru
38tl, Mark Kostich 18bl; **Shutterstock.com:** Colorsport 34; **Victory Gallop:** T. Stevens / Akron Children's Hospital 37tr, 40b, 41t, 41br,
42-43t, Toril Simon 37b, 38b, 39tl, 39cr, 43tr, 43br

Cover images: *Front and Spine:* **Dreamstime.com:** Slowmotionglil

All other images © Dorling Kindersley
For more information see: www.dkimages.com

For the curious
www.dk.com

Horse
Heroes

Kate Petty and Paige Towler

CONTENTS

Pegasus
In Greek mythology, Pegasus was a beautiful winged horse who became a constellation of stars in the sky.

HORSES IN HISTORY

People and horses have always had a special relationship. Ever since horses were first tamed and ridden 6,000 years ago, they have been admired for their intelligence, strength, and speed.

In ancient Greece, a beautiful, well-trained horse was the ultimate status symbol of kings and generals. The conqueror Alexander the Great was so proud of his brave horse Bucephalus (Byoo-SEFF-uh-luss) that he named a city after him.

Statue of Alexander the Great riding Bucephalus in battle

People of the Roman Empire loved the drama of horse racing. They flocked to the arena to watch their favorite chariot teams thundering around the racetrack.

For centuries, horses have also been important to Indigenous peoples in North America. The tribes of the Great Plains were expert horsepeople and relied on horses for hunting buffalo and carrying warriors into battle.

Wherever people and horses have worked together, they have formed a loyal bond. This book tells the stories of some remarkable horses who have worked with their human partners to become heroes.

Chariots
Roman chariot races were dangerous and exciting. Crashes were common.

A Dakota Sioux warrior and a Pawnee warrior battle on horseback.

UNITED STATES

California

Missouri

Long Journey
Johnny Fry traveled 2,000 miles (3,200 km) from Missouri to California.

First Delivery
Johnny Fry's mail sack held 49 letters and 3 newspapers.

PONY EXPRESS

When the little mustang came into view, the crowd began to clap and cheer.

Her rider, Johnny Fry, led her into the packed town square of St. Joseph, Missouri, USA, that warm April evening in 1860. Johnny checked the mail pouch on the mustang's back for the last time as she snorted excitedly.

This poster for the Pony Express service dates from 1861.

The cost of sending a letter on the Pony Express was based on the letter's weight.

Mustang
This hardy breed is descended from the horses that Spanish explorers brought to the Americas.

A cannon boomed. The mustang left the cheering crowds behind. Horse and rider had entered history as the first ever Pony Express team.

In 1860 there were no telephones and computers. The latest news was delivered through the mail, and it could take more than a month for letters and newspapers to travel across the United States by wagon.

The Pony Express was a horse relay designed to keep the mail moving day and night. Mail could reach California from Missouri in just 10 days.

Each horse galloped at top speed to the next station. The mail was transferred to a fresh horse and the rider galloped off again on his new mount. Riders changed horses about six to eight times.

Express Riders
Pony Express riders had to be under 18 years old and weigh less than 126 pounds (57 kg), so as not to slow down their horses.

9

Lincoln
In 1860, Abraham Lincoln's first speech as U.S. president was carried by the Pony Express.

Stagecoach
The Pony Express closed down when the transcontinental telegraph system opened in 1861. Stagecoach operators Wells, Fargo & Company took over the route.

The Pony Express teams rode across rocky mountain passes and wide, empty plains in scorching sun, pouring rain, and freezing blizzards. If their rider fell off, some brave horses carried on alone to the next station.

The final stop was Sacramento, California. Crowds of eager people would gather to watch the arrival of the last rider on the route bringing them their mail and newspapers.

The success of the Pony Express teams proved that it was possible for the east and west coasts to keep in touch. It was a milestone on the way to modern America. The horses and riders that ran the Pony Express were real pioneers.

The Pony Express is remembered today by horse lovers who ride the express's desert tracks for pleasure. Their journeys pay tribute to the riders of 1860, who insisted that "the mail must get through."

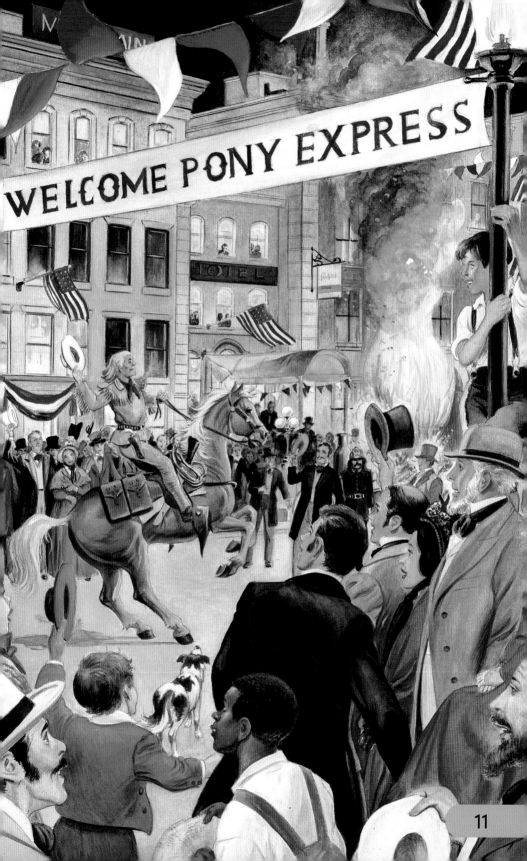

Tschiffely
Aimé Tschiffely
(Ay-may
Shiff-ell-ee)
was a Swiss
teacher living
in Argentina.

UNITED STATES

Washington, D.C.

Buenos Aires
ARGENTINA

Americas
Tschiffely
wanted to ride
from South to
North America
across the
Panama Canal.

TALE OF TWO HORSES

When Tschiffely told people about his idea early in 1925, they couldn't believe it.

"Impossible! It can't be done!"

Tschiffely wanted to be the first person ever to ride from Buenos Aires in Argentina all the way to Washington, D.C.

He realized that the 10,000-mile (16,000-km) journey would be full of difficulties, but it had been his secret ambition for years.

Tschiffely knew that he needed two tough and resourceful horses if he was to succeed. He chose Gato and Mancha, Criollo horses aged 15 and 16. They had roamed free on the plains. They were headstrong and knew how to survive in the wild.

Tschiffely and the horses set off in April 1925. After four months, the travelers crossed over into Bolivia. In that time the trio had learned to trust each other and to work together as a team.

One day, as they rode along the shore of a lake in Peru they reached a shallow strip of water. Gato reared up and refused to go on.

A man rushed toward them, shouting that the water hid dangerous quicksand. He led them to a safe trail. Tschiffely was amazed. The horse had saved their lives!

Criollo
These horses are very tough and can carry heavy weights over long distances.

As they rode on through Peru, they began to climb the Andes—a huge range of snowcapped mountains.

One morning, they came across a sight that made Tschiffely's blood run cold. The way forward was along a rickety old rope bridge that stretched over a deep gorge. One slip would prove fatal.

Tschiffely and Mancha slowly began to cross. Tschiffely spoke to his horse in a quiet, calm voice, gently patting its haunches.

When they reached the middle, the bridge swayed violently. If Mancha panicked and turned back, they would both fall to their deaths. But Mancha waited calmly for the bridge to stop moving, then went on. When Gato saw his companions safe on the other side, he crossed the bridge as steadily as if he were walking on solid ground.

Andes
The Andes stretch up to 20,000 feet (6,000 m) high. They are pitted with sheer, rocky gorges.

Rope Bridge
Andes natives have built thin rope bridges across gorges for centuries. Many people have to cross blindfolded because they are too scared to look down.

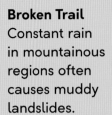

Broken Trail
Constant rain in mountainous regions often causes muddy landslides.

From Peru, Tschiffely headed into Ecuador and followed a series of tracks through lush forests over high mountains and down into valleys.

16

At night, Tschiffely never tied up the horses. He knew they would not run. The three travelers were sharing a great adventure, each showing the others the way.

Zigzagging up a narrow trail one day, Tschiffely saw that the path ahead had been swept away by a landslide, leaving a sheer drop. There was no choice but to turn back and find another route. Tschiffely tightened Gato's packs to get ready for a long detour.

But Mancha had other ideas. Tschiffely saw with horror that Mancha was preparing to jump the gap. His heart rose in his mouth as Mancha sailed through the air and landed on the other side. The horse turned and neighed to his companions not to be afraid. Tschiffely and Gato soon followed.

Herd Instincts
Wild horses stay in groups, or herds. Mancha and Gato would instinctively follow each other, whatever the dangers.

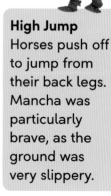

High Jump
Horses push off to jump from their back legs. Mancha was particularly brave, as the ground was very slippery.

Dense Jungle
The jungles of Central and South America are home to some of the world's most dangerous snakes, such as the 30–foot (10-m) anaconda.

Crocodile
Horses seem to remember that their ancestors were hunted by crocodiles, and know to be afraid of them.

As their adventure stretched on, the three travelers reached the Panama Canal and crossed into Costa Rica and then Mexico.

Moving through dense jungle, the trio had to cope with mosquito bites and attacks by vampire bats and poisonous snakes.

Once, Mancha slipped into a crocodile-infested river. He only just managed to find a foothold and pull himself up the bank as Tschiffely clung on for dear life.

Two and a half years after setting out from Buenos Aires, Tschiffely reached Washington, D.C. He had achieved his lifelong ambition.

"I could never have done it," he said, "without Mancha and Gato. My two pals have shown powers of resistance to every hardship."

Tschiffely was given a hero's welcome, even meeting President Calvin Coolidge in the White House. Admirers suggested that the horses should live in a city park. But Tschiffely took Mancha and Gato back to Argentina and set them free.

TSCHIFFELY'S RIDE

BEING
THE ACCOUNT OF
10,000 MILES IN THE SADDLE
THROUGH THE AMERICAS
FROM ARGENTINA TO
WASHINGTON

BY
A. F. TSCHIFFELY

Tschiffely's Ride
Now a famous man, Aimé Tschiffely wrote a book about his adventures.

Born Free
Horses that grow up in the country can become sad and listless if confined in a city.

Movie Town
The 1930s was the golden age of filmmaking in Hollywood, California, USA.

Decked Out
Trigger's silver saddle cost $50,000 and was set with 1,000 rubies.

Trigger presents his passport for inspection on arrival in England in 1954.

HOLLYWOOD HERO

In 1932 a star was born. Son of a palomino mare and a racehorse, Golden Cloud was a beautiful golden color with a white, flowing mane and tail.

A famous singing cowboy actor, Roy Rogers, auditioned many horses for a series of Westerns in 1938. But he fell for Golden Cloud the moment he climbed onto the horse's back.

The horse was renamed "Trigger" because he was so quick. Trigger loved the camera and became one of the most popular characters onscreen. He knew over 60 tricks.

He could walk 150 steps on his hind legs and stamp his hoof to count.

Perfect Partners
Roy Rogers was called the King of the Cowboys, and Trigger soon became known as the Smartest Horse in the Movies.

Famous Pose
Trigger's most spectacular feat was rearing up on his back legs with Roy Rogers on his back.

Trigger always traveled in style, carried his own horse-sized passport, and signed his name with an X in hotel registers.

Trigger finally retired in 1957, and died in 1965, aged 33. Roy Rogers was heartbroken. He said he had lost "the greatest horse who ever came along."

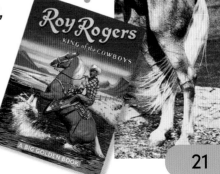

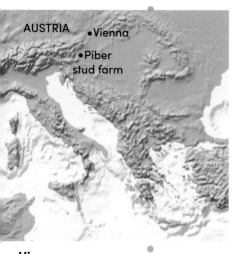

AUSTRIA •Vienna

•Piber
stud farm

Vienna
The Spanish
Riding School of
Vienna, Austria,
was founded
in 1572. It is
called "Spanish"
because the
original horses
in the school
were from Spain.

BALLET ON HORSEBACK

"He's a lively one," said the boy working in the stable. pointing toward the dark colt leading the race across the field.

The colt's name was Favory. He was one of the Lipizzaner foals born in the early 1980s at the Piber stud farm, where horses are bred for the Spanish Riding School.

Lipizzaner foals, or young horses, run free on the Piber stud farm.

"Look how much energy he's got," said the boy.

"Maybe too much," said one of the grooms. Favory was popular with the workers at the stud farm, but could he make it at the school? The groom knew that if Favory was going to perform at the school's regular displays, he had to have personality, discipline, and strength.

Lipizzaner
The school's horses are Lipizzaners. They are descended from six stallions, one of which was called Favory. His descendants are always given his name.

Lipizzaners are born with dark hair, but it usually turns white when they are about two years old.

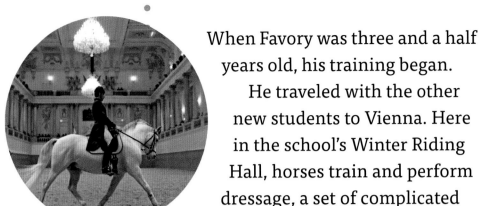

When Favory was three and a half years old, his training began.

He traveled with the other new students to Vienna. Here in the school's Winter Riding Hall, horses train and perform dressage, a set of complicated steps that have been the same for centuries. The school is famous worldwide for how skillfully its horses can do dressage.

Arena
The grand Winter Riding Hall was built in 1735 by Emperor Charles VI of Austria. His portrait hangs at the far end of the arena.

Hardest of all the steps are the "Airs above the ground," a series of amazing jumps that only the strongest horses can perform. All the riders at the school were eager to see if any of the new students were strong and steady enough to make the grade.

Unfortunately, Favory didn't give a good first impression. He broke away from his groom and galloped around the hall, showing off.

"We've got our work cut out with that one," said one of the riders.

Watching Favory closely was the First Chief Rider, the most experienced rider in the school. He liked horses with spirit. But did Favory have the self-control that he would need to perform the Airs? There was only one way to find out.

Riders
Riders join the school as teenagers and spend six years training. A Chief Rider must have taught at least one horse the Airs.

Costume
Riders wear hats, tailcoats, and high black boots.

In Hand
A lunge rope is used to teach a horse to move in a controlled way and to obey the voice of its human.

Equipment
The school has its own saddler to maintain the tack (saddles and bridles), some of which is hundreds of years old. Saddles are traditionally made out of white deerskin.

The First Chief Rider decided to train Favory himself. He wanted to get the best out of Favory without changing his unique character.

For the first two weeks, the First Chief Rider led Favory gently by hand. Then he put a saddle on Favory and trained him on a rope called a lunge.

The First Chief Rider put the saddle on Favory for just a few minutes at a time, so that the horse could get used to it. Soon, Favory let the First Chief Rider get on the saddle and ride him.

Then, the First Chief Rider taught Favory how to focus his energy into performing dressage steps.

In just a few years, Favory was good enough to perform in the dressage section of the school's shows.

The school's shows are famous all over the world. The horses and riders perform dressage, the Airs, and a ballet to music.

The First Chief Rider was pleased with Favory's progress in the shows. Now it was time for the hardest task of all—to teach Favory the Airs.

Back View
Lipizzaners' tails may be braided for performances.

Levade
(Leh-vad)
The horse raises its front legs up to six feet (2 m) off the ground.

Courbette
(Cur-bet)
This involves jumping forward in the *Levade* position.

The first Air that Favory learned was the *Levade*. He had to rear up and balance on his hind legs.

Strongly built horses go on to learn the *Courbette*. But Favory's lively personality made him ideally suited for the *Capriole*.

To perform this spectacular Air, Favory had to leap up with all four feet off the ground. Then, at the highest point of the jump he had to kick his back legs out behind him.

Favory practiced the Airs until he could do them perfectly every time. It was not long before the First Chief Rider gave him a wonderful reward.

As the show draws to a close, the First Chief Rider presents a fully trained horse to demonstrate the *Capriole*. It must be a horse with great talent and a calm mind.

"Let's go," said the First Chief Rider one evening to the horse that he had chosen.

The audience gasped as a magnificent horse trotted gracefully to the center of the arena.

It was Favory. At last he had the chance to show off his skills. He performed the Airs to perfection and the audience loved him. Favory was a star.

Capriole
(Cap-ree-ol)
This movement was developed for army horses to scare their enemies on the battlefield. It is often done in performance on a lunge rope.

Show Jumping
Show jumping is a competitive equestrian event. Horses that compete must jump over obstacles such as fences within a time limit.

STROLLER STEALS THE SHOW

During a warm October in 1968, the Olympic Games were underway in Mexico City, Mexico. A bay horse named Stroller was getting ready to compete in show jumping with his rider, Marion Coakes. But Stroller wasn't like the other horses competing—he was much smaller. In fact, at about 4.7 feet (1.4 m) tall, he was considered a pony. Ponies had never competed at the Olympics in show jumping before. But Coakes was confident that Stroller could do it. After all, the duo had already done amazing things together.

Born in England in 1947, Coakes had grown up in a family of horse riders. She met Stroller when she was 13 years old, and she had been riding for years. The 10-year-old Stroller hadn't really won any important competitions. But right away, Coakes could tell that he was special. In fact, when Coakes's father suggested getting a larger horse for competitions, she refused; she and Stroller were a pair.

Olympic Games
Although the Olympics date back to the eighth century BCE, the first modern Olympic Games were held in Athens in 1896.

Marion Coakes with Stroller

Bay Coloring
Horses with bay coloring typically have reddish-brown coats with black "points" on their mane, tail, upper ears, and lower legs.

Soon, Stroller and Coakes were entering events together. Many people didn't think the pony could keep pace with the larger horses. They had more powerful muscles and longer legs for jumping. But Stroller proved those people wrong. In 1962, Stroller won the Queen Elizabeth II Cup in Britain's Royal International Horse Show. Then, the incredible pony won three events at the Longines FEI Jumping Nations Cup! He also placed second in the final of the Hickstead Derby in West Sussex, England, one of the world's most difficult courses.

In 1965, Stroller and Coakes entered—and won—the Ladies' World Championship. Two years later, they returned to the Hickstead Derby. This time, they won.

Cheering fans greeted Stroller and Coakes at the Olympic Games in 1968. People all over the world had taken notice of the amazing pony and his rider. But something was wrong: Stroller was suffering from a split upper tooth. There was no time to operate before the Games. Would he be able to compete?

Show Jumping Attire
When competing in show jumping events, riders traditionally wear tall black boots, fitted pants called breeches, tailored jackets, and protective headgear.

Origins
Show jumping likely originated in Europe in the late 17th century and quickly became popular in countries such as France, Ireland, and Italy.

As it turns out, Stroller didn't just compete. Even with an injured tooth, he sailed to second place, earning a silver medal. More than that, he had made history: Stroller was the first pony to compete in show jumping at the Olympics. But Stroller and Coakes didn't stop there. In 1970, the pair was victorious in Germany's Hamburg Derby, making Coakes the first female rider, and Stroller the first pony, to win. The team had proved to the world that they could not only compete with the big horses—they could win.

Hamburg Derby
Also known as the German Jumping and Dressage Derby, the Hamburg Derby has been running in Hamburg since 1869.

Shetland Ponies
A Shetland pony is a breed of horse from Scotland's Shetland Islands. The breed is known for its short legs and strength.

Miniature Horses
A miniature horse is a breed of horse that has been bred to be very small. Miniature horses are usually under 34 inches (86 cm) tall.

PETIE THE PONY

There are many ways to be a hero. For one special horse, this meant helping others in the best way he knew how—by being kind.

Petie the Pony was part Shetland pony, part miniature horse. He was very small. Unlike most horses, which are often taller than adult humans, Petie was about the size of a very large dog. But Petie's small size wouldn't stop him from having a huge impact. This was especially clear to two women, Sue Miller and Kim Gustely.

In 1995, Miller and Gustely founded a nonprofit program called Victory Gallop, located in Ohio, USA. This organization aimed to provide therapeutic horseback riding for kids with behavioral or emotional challenges and life-threatening illnesses. By riding horses or helping take care of them, children can increase their physical strength, gain confidence, and enjoy themselves.

But Victory Gallop also wanted to help children and other people who might not be able to ride horses at all.

When Victory Gallop adopted Petie, she knew he was special. Petie was quiet and calm. He was incredibly patient and very gentle. The team at Victory Gallop had an idea: when kids couldn't come to the horses, why not bring the horses to them?

Therapeutic Something that is therapeutic is meant to provide healing or therapy for certain illnesses or conditions.

Horse Training
One technique for training horses is called longeing. Longeing exercises keep horses healthy and help them learn to walk in ways that are safe for their body. Longeing also teaches them how to safely change between different speeds.

Precious Ponies
Therapy ponies know to be very gentle and patient with the people they are visiting. Sometimes, Petie would gently rest his head by a patient if they couldn't get out of bed.

Petie began his training right away. He learned how to walk in and out of many different small rooms. He practiced spending time around loud noises to make sure they didn't spook him. Over time, he even learned to walk through revolving doors and ride up elevators. But that wasn't all: Petie had to learn how to be housebroken, too. Luckily, he was a very smart horse—he learned how to let his handlers know that he needed to take a bathroom break. Soon, Petie was ready to make the team's idea a reality.

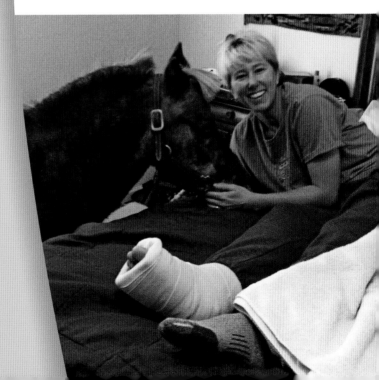

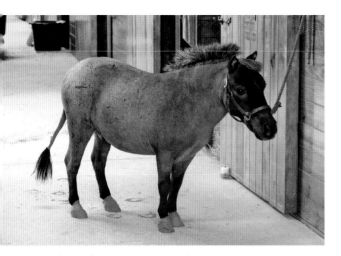

This horse's hooves and tail get wrapped up just like Petie's did.

Bathtime
Bathing a horse helps get rid of any dirt that has built up in the horse's coat or tail. It also helps a horse shed hair from its coat.

In 1997, Petie began to visit patients at hospitals. Before each trip, he spent a long time getting ready to make sure everything would be safe for the children. First, Petie's team gave him not one, but two—or sometimes three—baths. Then, they scrubbed each of Petie's hooves and conditioned his long tail. They also dried each hoof and wrapped it up to make sure it stayed clean, and wrapped up his tail as well. Petie was a remarkably patient horse through the whole process! Once Petie reached the hospital, his team removed his wrappings and cleaned his nose. Then, his real work began.

Travel
Like they did with Petie, to get this horse from one place to another, his team transports him in a special type of vehicle known as a horse trailer.

39

Motor Skills
Motor skills include the body's ability to move. Fine motor skills refer to the more detailed movements, such as using fingers.

Petie visited children in the hospital who were injured or sick. Many of these children were in pain. Others often felt scared, bored, sad, or alone. Petie was the hero they needed. When Petie entered a room, he would patiently let the children stroke his soft head and mane. Sometimes, he nuzzled their hands or breathed softly to help calm them down. Other times, the children brushed Petie's silky coat or helped put on his harness, which let them strengthen their motor skills.

One of the Pack
Many people train dogs to be therapy animals. When Petie first started visiting patients, he joined a group known as the Doggy Brigade.

A Hero for All
Petie also visited nursing homes and schools. He not only comforted adults and kids, but he also helped teach them about horses.

Fun Tricks
Some horses can be taught to use their long necks to "hug" people—or to give them a "kiss" on the cheek!

No matter what they did together, Petie's presence helped cheer up the children. Kids adored Petie's big, brown eyes, and they were delighted to see a real horse in a hospital—of all places!

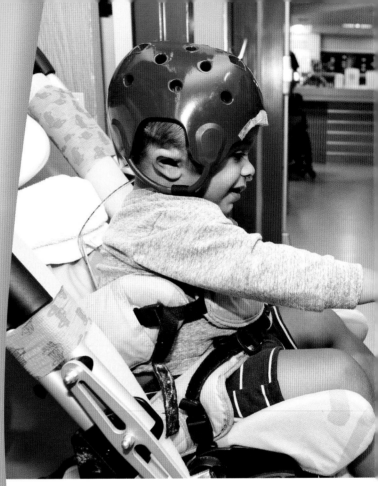

A Birthday for Petie

For Petie's 25th birthday, his handlers threw him a party—complete with party hats, lots of pets, and the happy birthday song played on a guitar.

Petie was the first therapeutic horse in the United States, and he helped people for more than 20 years. But he was not the last. Although Petie passed away in 2017, his legacy lives on. Petie remains a hero for many people. He has also inspired the team at Victory Gallop to train another therapy horse to follow in Petie's hoofsteps.

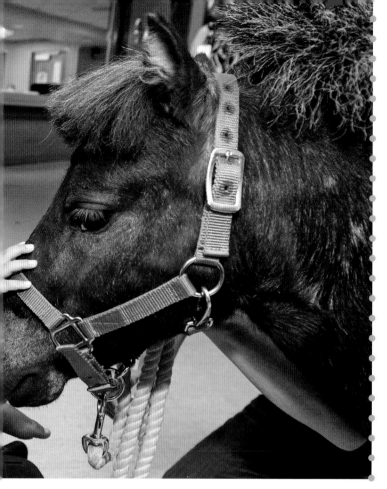

Since 2018, a miniature horse named Willie Nelson has been continuing Petie's work by visiting hospitals, nursing homes, and schools to bring comfort and cheer to people who need it.

Like Petie, Willie Nelson is a small horse with a huge heart full of kindness. And also like Petie, Willie Nelson proves that sometimes, kindness is all it takes to be a hero.

Famous Horses
Both Petie and Willie Nelson have been featured in magazine articles, on news channels, and even on talk shows.

Stuffie
After a visit from Willie Nelson, each patient receives a small, stuffed horse that looks like Willie. This helps them remember their special meeting.

Przewalski horse

Wild ass

Hands High
The height of a horse is measured in "hands." One hand is the width of an adult's hand— about four inches (10 cm).

THE HORSE FAMILY

Horses and ponies belong to the same family as donkeys, wild asses, and zebras. This is called the Equid (ECK-wid) family.

In the wild, horses live in herds on open grasslands. They use speed to escape from their enemies, and newborn foals can get up and run within an hour of being born.

Horses form strong bonds with other members of their herd. This loyalty is easily transferred to a human owner.

Donkey

Zebra

Heavy Horse
Heavy horses are tall and have broad, strong shoulders.

Light Horse
Light horses have narrow bodies, long legs, and sloped shoulders.

Pony
Ponies have shorter legs in relation to their bodies than light and heavy horses.

Domestic horses come in many different shapes and sizes, but there are three main types—heavy horses, light horses, and ponies. Heavy horses are the largest and can measure over 67 inches (168 cm) high. Ponies are the smallest and always measure under 58 inches (147 cm).

The oldest breed of horse is the Przewalski (perz-uh-VOL-skee) horse, which comes from Mongolia in Asia. It is the only living link with the wild ancestors of today's horses and ponies.

GLOSSARY

Ambition
Something that is strongly desired

Arena
An enclosed space for large shows and sporting events

Bay
A horse with a reddish coat and black mane, tail, legs, ears, and nose

Colt
A young male horse

Detour
A route taken when another route is blocked

Gorge
A deep valley, often with a river running through it

Groom
A person who looks after horses

Mare
A female horse

Mosquito
A small winged insect that bites

Palomino
A horse with a gold-colored coat and a white mane and tail

Passport
An official paper given to a person by the government so that the person can be identified in a foreign country

Quicksand
A deep, wet bed of sand that sucks down anything on its surface

Relay
A system where fresh runners or horses are posted at intervals along a route. Each member of a relay team runs only one part of the route.

Salute
Raising the right hand to the forehead to show respect

Stagecoach
A horse-drawn passenger coach that travels a regular route

Stallion
A fully grown male horse that can be used for breeding

Telegraph
A system for sending messages over long distances. It uses electronic signals sent through a wire.

Trotting sound
To run slowly and smoothly without limping

Vampire bat
A bat from Central or South America that lives on the blood of other animals

Western
A film about cowboys in the western United States, especially during the time of exploration

White House
The large white building in Washington, D.C. that is home to the president of the United States

INDEX

QUIZ

Answer the questions to see what you have learned. Check your answers in the key below.

1. What did Alexander the Great name after his horse?

2. True or False: Pony Express riders rode the same horse from station to station.

3. Aimé Tschiffely wanted to be the first person to do what?

4. What was the name of Roy Rogers's horse?

5. What are the hardest steps in dressage?

6. How was Stroller different from the other horses he competed with?

7. Where did Petie the Pony go to visit children?

8. What is the name of the family to which horses belong?

1. A city 2. False 3. To ride horses from Buenos Aires, Argentina, to Washington, D.C. 4. Trigger 5. The Airs 6. He was much smaller 7. Hospitals 8. Equid family